Encouragement for
the Depressed

The Crossway Short Classics Series

Encouragement for the Depressed
CHARLES SPURGEON

The Expulsive Power of a New Affection
THOMAS CHALMERS

Heaven Is a World of Love
JONATHAN EDWARDS

ENCOURAGEMENT
FOR THE
DEPRESSED

CHARLES SPURGEON

WHEATON, ILLINOIS

Cover design: Jordan Singer

Cover image: "Single Stem" wallpaper design, William Morris (1834–1896), Bridgeman Images

First printing 2020

Printed in China

Paperback ISBN: 978-1-4335-7063-6
ePub ISBN: 978-1-4335-7066-7
PDF ISBN: 978-1-4335-7064-3
Mobipocket ISBN: 978-1-4335-7065-0

Library of Congress Cataloging-in-Publication Data

Names: Spurgeon, C. H. (Charles Haddon), 1834–1892, author.
Title: Encouragement for the depressed / Charles Spurgeon.
Description: Wheaton, Illinois: Crossway, 2020. | Series: The Crossway short classics series | Includes bibliographical references and index.
Identifiers: LCCN 2020005166 (print) | LCCN 2020005167 (ebook) | ISBN 9781433570636 (trade paperback) | ISBN 9781433570643 (pdf) | ISBN 9781433570650 (mobi) | ISBN 9781433570667 (epub)
Subjects: LCSH: Depressed persons—Religious life. | Depression, Mental—Religious aspects—Christianity. | Depression, Mental—Biblical teaching.
Classification: LCC BV4910.34 .S695 2020 (print) | LCC BV4910.34 (ebook) | DDC 248.8/6—dc23
LC record available at https://lccn.loc.gov/2020005166
LC ebook record available at https://lccn.loc.gov/2020005167

Crossway is a publishing ministry of Good News Publishers.

RRDS   28 27 26 25 24 23 22 21 20
14 13 12 11 10 9 8 7 6 5 4 3 2 1

Contents

Foreword

HARDLY ANYONE OUTSIDE of Scripture speaks
to me like Charles Spurgeon does. He had incred-
ible depth and biblical insight, and his sermons
and writings, full of grace and truth and sheer
eloquence, always draw me to Jesus.

Spurgeon preached to approximately ten mil-
lion people in his lifetime, often speaking ten times
a week. His 3,561 sermons are bound in sixty-three
volumes, and in addition he wrote many books.

Wonderful as those accomplishments were,
they put demands on his life that no doubt con-
tributed to his battles with depression—not least
of all that he often worked eighteen hours a day!

Spurgeon took great solace in Scripture, especially in the Psalms he loved so much, as evidenced in his massive commentary set *The Treasury of David*. God's words, as Spurgeon well knew, are far more valuable than anyone else's. God promises that his word "shall not return to [him] empty, but it shall accomplish that which [he purposes], and shall succeed in the thing for which [he] sent it" (Isa. 55:11 ESV). God does not make that promise about your words or my words or even Spurgeon's words, but only his word. In the face of great criticism, Spurgeon took great pains to conform his preaching and writing to Scripture. We need to hear Spurgeon's voice because he was faithful to speak God's word, and today there aren't nearly enough voices like his.

Spurgeon also serves as a reminder that people of great trust in God can nonetheless be brought low in depression. While that thought may be, well, depressing to those who haven't experienced depression, it is liberating to those of us who have.

I have known depression at times in my life. Several years ago, for no apparent reason, a cloud of depression descended on me. Day after day, it was my constant companion. During that time, I was encouraged by the perspectives of Spurgeon, whose long-term struggles with depression were far worse than mine. I blogged about my depression and shared a few Spurgeon quotations that can be found in this book.

Many people have since written to tell me their own stories of how God has used Spurgeon's perspectives on depression in their lives. After I wrote a subsequent blog post about Spurgeon and the suffering he endured, I received this note: "I was depressed because once again I was not feeling well. It's amazing to realize even great leaders suffered so much. It gives me hope, as I suffer from near constant pain. Thanks. This really encouraged me—I needed it!"

Would Spurgeon have ever guessed that nearly two centuries later his sufferings from depression would be a source of comfort to God's people? (Who is being, and will be, touched by our sufferings and our perspectives that we won't know about until eternity?) I am confident that God will use Spurgeon's words in this little book to encourage many more believers who struggle with depression.

Spurgeon writes, "I have suffered many times from severe sickness and frightful mental depression sinking almost to despair. Almost every year I've been laid aside for a season, for flesh and blood cannot bear the strain, at least such flesh and blood as mine. [However,] I believe . . . that affliction was necessary to me and has answered salutary ends."[1]

Those words were written by a man who lived with great physical pain for a large part of his life. While his dear wife, Susanna, was bedridden for decades, Spurgeon contracted smallpox and suffered from gout, rheumatism, and Bright's disease (inflammation of the kidneys). His health became progressively worse, so that nearly a third of his last twenty-two years were spent away from the pulpit. This physical hardship took a great emotional toll on him.

When Spurgeon was twenty-two years old, a tragedy took place that still haunted him years later. He was preaching for the first time in the Music Hall of the Royal Surrey Gardens because his own church

---

1   From an address by Spurgeon on May 19, 1879. Cited in Ernest LeVos, *C. H. Spurgeon and the Metropolitan Tabernacle* (iUniverse, 2014), 48.

wasn't large enough. The ten-thousand-person seating capacity was far exceeded by the crowds pressing in. Someone shouted, "Fire!" and though there was no fire, the resulting stampede caused many injuries and the deaths of seven people. Years later, Spurgeon said this horrifying incident took him "near the burning furnace of insanity."[2]

Still, Spurgeon found that his great suffering drew him closer to God. In an address to ministers and students, he said, "I daresay the greatest earthly blessing that God can give to any of us is health, *with the exception of sickness*. . . . If some men that I know of could only be favoured with a month of rheumatism, it would, by God's grace, mellow them marvelously."[3]

---

2 Charles Spurgeon, cited in *Great Preaching on the Deity of Christ*, comp. Curtis Hutson (Murfreesboro, TN: Sword of the Lord, 2000), 206.

3 Charles Spurgeon, *An All-Round Ministry* (Edinburgh: Banner of Truth, 1960), 384.

As you'll see in the pages that follow, Spurgeon said of pastoral ministry,

Our work, when earnestly undertaken, lays us open to attacks in the direction of depression. Who can bear the weight of souls without sometimes sinking to the dust? Passionate longings after men's conversion, if not fully satisfied (and when are they?), consume the soul with anxiety and disappointment. To see the hopeful turn aside, the godly grow cold, professors abusing their privileges, and sinners waxing more bold in sin—are not these sights enough to crush us to the earth. . . . How often, on Lord's Day evenings, do we feel as if life were completely washed out of us! After pouring out our souls over our congregations, we feel like empty earthen pitchers that a child might break.

He also wrote, "I am afraid that all the grace I have got of my comfortable and easy times and happy hours, might almost lie on a penny. But the good that I have received from my sorrows, and pains, and griefs, is altogether incalculable. . . . Affliction is . . . the best book in a minister's library."[4]

Like the apostle Paul, the often jovial Spurgeon was "sorrowful, yet always rejoicing" (2 Cor. 6:10 ESV). Near the end of his words that you're about to read, Spurgeon says, "Glory be to God for the furnace, the hammer, and the file. Heaven shall be all the fuller of bliss because we have been filled with anguish here below, and earth shall be better tilled because of our training in the school of adversity."

Thank you, Charles Spurgeon, for your integrity, devotion to God's word, honest sharing of

4 Charles Spurgeon, cited in Darrel W. Amundsen, "The Anguish and Agonies of Charles Spurgeon," in *Christian History* 29, no. 1 (1991): 25.

your own weaknesses, and unquenchable passion for God not just in times of good cheer, but in times of desolate darkness. And thank you, sovereign Lord, for encouraging us through your servant, who, like Abel, though he is dead (while fully alive in your presence), still speaks through his example and life-giving words (Heb. 11:4).

May God give us ears to hear, and may our hearts be full of hope and expectancy as we await the day when King Jesus, true to his blood-bought promise, will wipe away every tear from our eyes (Rev. 21:4).

Randy Alcorn
Founder and director,
Eternal Perspective Ministries

Series Preface

JOHN PIPER ONCE WROTE that books do not change people, but paragraphs do. This pithy statement gets close to the idea at the heart of the Crossway Short Classics series: some of the greatest and most powerful Christian messages are also some of the shortest and most accessible. The broad stream of confessional Christianity contains an astonishing wealth of timeless sermons, essays, lectures, and other short pieces of writing. These pieces have challenged, inspired, and borne fruit in the lives of millions of believers across church history and around the globe.

The Crossway Short Classics series seeks to serve two purposes. First, it aims to beautifully preserve these short historic pieces of writing through new high-quality physical editions. Second, it aims to transmit them to a new generation of readers, especially readers who may not be inclined or able to access a larger volume. Short-form content is especially valuable today, as the challenge of focusing in a distracting, constantly moving world becomes more intense. The volumes in the Short Classics series present incisive, gospel-centered grace and truth through a concise, memorable medium. By connecting readers with these accessible works, the Short Classics series hopes to introduce Christians to those great heroes of the faith who wrote them, providing readers with representative works that both nourish the soul and inspire further study.

Readers should note that the spelling and punctuation of these works have been lightly updated where applicable. Scripture references and other citations have also been added where appropriate. Language that reflects a work's origin as a sermon or public address has been retained. Our goal is to preserve as much as possible the authentic text of these classic works.

Our prayer is that the Holy Spirit will use these short works to arrest your attention, preach the gospel to your soul, and motivate you to continue exploring the treasure chest of church history, to the praise and glory of God in Christ.

Biography of
Charles Spurgeon

CHARLES HADDON SPURGEON (1834–1892) was one of the greatest Baptist preachers and theologians of the nineteenth century. Born June 19, 1834, in England, Spurgeon was converted to genuine Christian faith at fifteen years of age, when, entering a church's Sunday service to get out of inclement weather, he heard a Methodist minister explain the gospel from Isaiah 45:22: "Look unto me, and be ye saved, all the ends of the earth." Spurgeon's preaching career began soon afterward, and at only nineteen he was called as pastor of London's largest Baptist church.

Spurgeon quickly became famous in London for the power of his preaching, which combined serious Reformed theology with passionate gospel pleas for the souls of his hearers. His sermons used the whole content of the Bible to point the audience to the all-satisfying, all-sufficient, all-important person and work of Christ. His unique blend of biblical insight, theological rigor, and practical exhortation and encouragement have helped Spurgeon endure as one of the most admired and influential gospel preachers in church history, earning him the affectionate title "The Prince of Preachers."

Spurgeon's work expanded far beyond the pulpit. He founded a pastor's college in 1856, where he taught and mentored hundreds of ministers. In addition to his published sermons, Spurgeon authored many books and delivered many lectures. Arguably his most famous works are his devotionals, which include *Morning and Evening* and *The Cheque Book of the Bank of Faith* (re-published in 2019 as *The Promises of God*). He also authored a three-volume commentary on the Psalms and published many theological essays. A tireless public theologian, Spurgeon engaged the pressing religious and cultural issues of his day, taking a stand for theological orthodoxy, personal evangelism, the care of orphans, and the abolition of slavery.

ENCOURAGEMENT

FOR THE

DEPRESSED

*"For who hath despised the
day of small things?"*

Zechariah 4:10

I

ZECHARIAH WAS ENGAGED in the building of the temple. When its foundations were laid, it struck everybody as being a very small edifice compared with the former glorious structure of Solomon. The friends of the enterprise lamented that it should be so small; the foes of it rejoiced and uttered strong expressions of contempt. Both friends and foes doubted whether, even on that small scale, the structure would ever be completed. They might lay the foundations, and they might rear the walls a little way, but they were too feeble a folk, possessed of too little riches and too little strength, to carry out the enterprise. It was the day of small things. Friends trembled; foes jeered. But the prophet rebuked them both—rebuked the unbelief of friends, and the contempt of enemies, by this question, "Who hath despised the day of small things?" and by a subsequent prophecy that removed the fear.

Now we shall use this question at this time for the comfort of two sorts of people—first, *for weak believers*, and second, *for feeble workers*. Our object shall be the strengthening of the hands that hang down and the confirming of the feeble knees.

Let us describe them. It is with them a day of small things. Probably you have only been lately brought into the family of God. A few months ago, you were a stranger to the divine life and to the things of God. You have been born again, and you have the weakness of the infant. You are not strong yet, as you will be when you have grown in grace and in the knowledge of our Lord and

Savior Jesus Christ. It is the early day with you, and it is also the day of small things.

Now your *knowledge* is small. My dear brother, you have not been a Bible student long: thank God that you know yourself a sinner, and Christ your Savior. That is precious knowledge; but you feel now what you once would not have confessed—your own ignorance of the things of God. Especially do the deep things of God trouble you. There are some doctrines that are very simple to other believers that appear to be mysterious, and even to be depressing to you. They are high—you cannot attain to them. They are to you what hard nuts would be to children whose teeth have not yet appeared.

Well, be not at all alarmed about this. All the men in God's family have once been children too. There are some that seem to be born with knowledge—Christians that come to a height in

Christ very rapidly. But these are only here and there. Israel did not produce a Samson every day. Most have to go through a long period of spiritual infancy and youth. And, alas! There are but few in the church, even now, who might be called fathers there. Do not marvel, therefore, if you are somewhat small in your knowledge.

Your *discernment*, too, is small. It is possible that anybody with a fluent tongue would lead you into error. You have, however, discernment, if you are a child of God, sufficient to be kept from deadly errors, for though there are some who would, if it were possible, deceive even the very elect, yet the elect cannot be deceived, for, the life of God being in them, they discern between the precious and the vile—they choose not the things of the world, but they follow after the things of God.

Your discernment, however, seeming so small, need not afflict you. It is by reason of use, when the senses are exercised, that we fully discern between all that is good and all that is evil. Thank God for a little discernment—though you see men as trees walking, and your eyes are only half opened. A little light is better than none at all. Not long since you were in total darkness. Now if there be a glimmer, be thankful, for remember that where a glimmer can enter, the full noontide can come, yea, and shall come in due season. Therefore, despise not the time of small discernment.

Of course, you, my dear brother or sister, have small *experience*. I trust you will not ape experience and try to talk as if you had the experience of the veteran saints when you are as yet only a raw recruit. You have not yet done business on the great waters. The more fierce temptations of Satan have not assailed you—the wind has been tempered as yet to the shorn lamb; God has not hung heavy weights on slender threads, but hath put a small burden on a weak back. Be thankful that it is so. Thank him for the experience that you have, and do not be desponding because you have not more. It will all come in due time.

Despise not the day of small things. It is always unwise to get down a biography and say, "Oh! I cannot be right, because I have not felt all this good man did." If a child of ten years of age were to take down the diary of his grandfather and were to say, "Because I do not feel my grandfather's weakness, do not require to use his spectacles or lean upon his staff, therefore I am not one of the same family," it would be very foolish reasoning. Your experience will ripen. As yet it is but natural that it should be green. Wait a while, and bless God for what you have.

Probably this, however, does not trouble you so much as one other thing, that you have but small *faith*, and, that faith being small, your feelings are very variable. I often hear this from young beginners in the divine life: "I was so happy a month ago, but I have lost that happiness now." Perhaps tomorrow, after they have been at the house of God, they will be as cheerful as possible, but the next day their joy will be gone. Beware, my dear Christian friends, of living by feeling. John Bunyan puts down Mr. Live-by-Feeling as one of the worst enemies of the town of Mansoul. I think he said he was hanged. I am afraid he, somehow or other, escaped from the executioner, for I very commonly meet him, and there is no villain that hates the souls of men and causes more sorrow to the people of God than this Mr. Live-by-Feeling.

He that lives by feeling will be happy today and unhappy tomorrow; and if our salvation depended upon our feelings, we should be lost one day and saved another, for they are as fickle as the weather, and go up and down like a barometer. We live by faith, and if that faith be weak, bless God that weak faith is faith, and that weak faith is true faith. If thou believest in Christ Jesus, though thy faith be as a grain of mustard seed, it will save thee, and it will, by and by, grow into something stronger. A diamond is a diamond, and the smallest scrap of it is of the same nature as the Koh-i-Noor,[1] and he that hath but little faith hath faith for all that; and it is not great faith that is essential to salvation, but faith that links the soul to Christ; and that soul is, therefore, saved.

Instead of mourning so much that thy faith is not strong, bless God that thou hast any faith at all, for if he sees that thou despisest the faith he has given thee, it may be long before he gives thee more. Prize that little, and when he sees that thou

---

1 At 105.6 carats, the Koh-i-Noor ("Mountain of Light") is among the world's largest cut diamonds. It is one of the British Crown Jewels.

art so glad and thankful for that little, then will he multiply it and increase it, and thy faith shall mount even to the full assurance of faith.

I think I hear you also add to all this the complaint that your *other graces* seem to be small too. "Oh," say you, "my patience is so little. If I have a little pain I begin to cry out. I was in hopes I should be able to bear it without murmuring. My courage is so little: the blush is on my cheek if anybody asks me about Christ—I think I could hardly confess him before half a dozen, much less before the world. I am very weak indeed." Ah! I don't wonder. I have known some who have been strong by reason of years, and have still been lacking in that virtue. But where faith is weak, of course, the rest will be weak. A plant that has a weak root will naturally have a weak stem and then will have but weak fruit. Your weakness of faith sends a weakness through the whole.

But for all this, though you are to seek for more faith, and consequently for more grace—for stronger graces—yet do not despise what graces you have. Thank God for them, and pray that the few clusters that are now upon you may be multiplied a thousandfold to the praise of the glory of his grace.

II

Thus, I have tried to describe those who are passing through the day of small things.

But the text says, *"Who hath despised the day of small things?"* Well, some have, but there is a great comfort in this—*God the Father* has not. He has looked upon you—you, with little grace, and little love, and little faith—and he has not despised you. No, God is always near the feeble saint. If I saw a young man crossing a common alone, I should not be at all astonished, and I should not look round for his father. But I saw today, as I went home, a very tiny little tot right out on the common, a pretty little girl, and I thought, "The father or mother are near somewhere." And truly there was the father behind a tree, whom I had not seen. I was as good as sure that the little thing was not there all alone. And when I see a little weak child of God, I feel sure that God the Father is near, watching with wakeful eye and tending with gracious care the feebleness of his newborn child. He does not despise you if you are resting on his promise. The humble and contrite have a word all to themselves in Scripture, that these he will not despise.

It is another sweet and consoling thought that *God the Son* does not despise the day of small things. Jesus Christ does not, for you remember this word: "He shall carry . . . them [the lambs] in his bosom" (Isa. 40:11). We put that which we most prize nearest our heart, and this is what Jesus does. Some of us, perhaps, have outgrown the state in which we were lambs, but to ride in that heavenly carriage of the Savior's bosom—we might well be content to go back and be lambs again. He does not despise the day of small things.

And it is equally consolatory to reflect that *the Holy Spirit* does not despise the day of small things, for he it is who, having planted in the heart the grain of mustard seed, watches over it till it becomes a tree. He it is who, having seen the newborn child of grace, doth nurse, and feed, and tend it until it comes to the stature of a perfect man in Christ Jesus. The blessed Godhead despises not the weak believer. O weak believer, be consoled by this.

Who is it, then, that may despise the day of small things? Perhaps *Satan* has told you and whispered in your ear that such little grace as yours is not worth having, that such an insignificant plant as you are will surely be rooted up. Now, let me tell you that Satan is a liar, for he himself does not despise the day of small things; and I am sure of that, because he always makes a dead set upon those who are just coming to Christ. As soon as ever he sees that the soul is a little wounded by conviction, as soon as ever he discovers that a heart begins to pray, he will assault it with fiercer temptations than ever. I have known him try to drive such a one to suicide, or to lead him into worse sin than he has ever committed before. This is because

Satan trembles when he sees The weakest saint upon his knees.[2]

He may tell you that the little grace in you is of no account, but he knows right well that it is the

2 From the hymn "What Various Hindrances We Meet" by William Cowper, 1779.

handful of corn on the top of the mountain, the fruit whereof shall shake like Lebanon. He knows it is the little grace in the heart that overthrows his kingdom there.

"Ah!" say you, "but I have been greatly troubled lately because I have many *friends* that despise me, because though I can hardly say I am a believer, yet I have some desire toward God." What sort of friends are these? Are they worldly friends? Oh! Do not fret about what they say. It would never trouble me, if I were an artist, if a blind man were to utter the sharpest criticism of my works. What does he know about it? And when an ungodly person begins to say about your piety that it is deficient and faulty, poor soul, let him say what he will—it need not affect you.

"Ah!" say you, "the persons that seem to despise me, and to put me out, and tell me that I am no child of God are, I believe, *Christians*." Well, then, do two things. First, lay what they say to you in a measure to heart, because it may be if God's children do not see in you the mark of a child, perhaps you are not a child. Let it lead you to examination. Oh! Dear friends, it is very easy to be self-deceived, and God may employ, perhaps, one of his servants to enlighten you upon this and deliver you from a strong delusion. But on the other hand, if you really do trust in your Savior, if you have begun to pray, if you have some love to God, and any Christian treats you harshly as if he thought you a hypocrite, forgive him—bear it. He has made a mistake. He would not do so if he knew you better. Say within yourself, "After all, if my brother does not know me, it is enough if my Father does. If my Father loves me, though my brother gives me the cold shoulder, I will be sorry for it, but it shall not break my heart. I will cling the closer to my Lord because his servants seem shy of me."

Why, it is not much wonder, is it, that some Christians should be afraid of some of you converts, for think what you used to be a little while ago? Why, a mother hears her son say he is converted. A month or two ago, she knew where he spent his evenings and what were his habits of sin, and though she hopes it is so, she is afraid lest she should lead him to presumption, and she rejoices with trembling and, perhaps, tells him more about her trembling than she does about her rejoicing.

Why, the saints of old could not think Saul was converted at first. He was to be brought into the church meeting and received—I will suppose the case. I should not wonder that before he came, when he saw the elders, one of them would say, "Well, the young man seems to know something of the grace of God: there is certainly a change in him, but it is a remarkable thing that he should wish to join the very people he was persecuting; but perhaps it is a mere impulse. It may be, after all, that he will go back to his old companions."

Do you wonder they should say so? I don't. I am not at all surprised. I am sorry when there are unjust suspicions, I am sorry when a genuine child of God is questioned; but I would not have you lay it much to heart. As I have said before, if your Father knows you, you need not be so broken in heart because your brother does not. Be glad that God does not despise the day of small things.

And now let me say to you who are in this state of small things, that I earnestly trust that you will not *yourselves* despise the day of small things. "How can we do that?" say you. Why, you can do it by *desponding.* Why, I think there was a time when you would have been ready to leap for joy if you had been told that you would be given a little faith, but now that you have got a little faith, instead of rejoicing, you are sighing, and moaning, and mourning. Do not do so. Be thankful for moonlight, and you shall get sunlight: be thankful for sunlight, and you shall get that light of heaven that is as the light of seven days. Do not despond lest you seem to despise the mercy that God has given you.

A poor patient that has been very, very lame and weak, and could not rise from his bed, is at last able to walk with a stick. "Well," he says to himself, "I wish I could walk, and run, and leap as other men." Suppose he sits down and frets because he cannot. His physician might put his hand on his shoulder and say, "My good fellow, why, you ought to be thankful you can stand at all. A little while ago, you know, you could not stand upright. Be glad for what you have got: don't seem to despise what has been done for you." I say to every Christian here, while you long after strength, don't seem to despise the grace that God has bestowed, but rejoice and bless his name.

You can despise the day of small things, again, by *not seeking after more.* "That is strange," say you. Well, a man who has got a little, and does not want more—it looks as if he despised the little. He who has a little light, and does not ask for more light, does not care for light at all. You that have a little faith, and do not want more faith, do not value faith at all—you are despising it. On the one hand, do not despond because you have the day of small things, but in the next place, *do not stand still and be satisfied with what you have;* but prove your value of the little by earnestly seeking after more grace.

Do not despise the grace that God has given you, but bless God for it: and do this in the presence of his people. If you hold your tongue about your grace and never let anyone know, surely it must be because you do not think it is worth saying anything about. Tell your brethren, tell your sisters, and they of the Lord's household that the Lord hath done gracious things for you; then it will be seen that you do not despise his grace.

And now let us run over a thought or two about these small things in weak believers. Be it remembered that little faith is saving faith, and that the day of small things is a day of safe things. Be it remembered that it is natural that living things should begin small. The man is first a babe. The daylight is first of all twilight. It is by little and by little that we come unto the stature of men in Christ Jesus. The day of small things is not only natural, but promising. Small things are living things. Let them alone, and they grow. The day of small things has its beauty and its excellence. I have known some who, in after years, would have liked to have gone back to their first days.

Oh! Well do some of us remember when we would have gone over hedge and ditch to hear a sermon. We had not much knowledge, but oh! how we longed to know. We stood in the aisles then, and we never got tired. Now soft seats we need, and very comfortable places, and the atmosphere must neither be too hot nor too cold. We are getting dainty now perhaps; but in those first young days of spiritual life, what appetites we had for divine truth, and what zeal, what sacred fire was in our hearts! True, some of it was wild fire and, perhaps, the energy of the flesh mingled with the power of the spirit, but, for all that, God remembers the love of our espousals, and so do we remember it too. The mother loves her grown-up son, but sometimes she thinks she does not love him as she did when she could cuddle him in her arms. Oh! the beauty of a little child! Oh! the beauty of a lamb in the faith! I daresay the farmer and the butcher like the sheep better than the lambs, but the lambs are best to look at, at any rate; and the rosebud—there is a charm about it that there is not in the full-blown rose.

And so, in the day of small things, there is a special excellence that we ought not to despise. Besides, small as grace may be in the heart, it is divine—it is a spark from the ever-blazing sun. He is a partaker of the divine nature who has even a little living faith in Christ. And being divine, it is immortal. Not all the devils in hell could quench the feeblest spark of grace that ever dropped into the heart of man. If God has given thee faith as a grain of mustard seed, it will defy all earth and hell, all time and eternity, ever to destroy it. So there is much reason why we should not despise the day of small things.

One word and I leave this point. You Christians, don't despise anybody, but specially do not despise any in whom you see even a little love to Christ. But do more—look after them, look after the little ones. I think I have heard of a shepherd who had a remarkably fine flock of sheep, and he had a secret about them. He was often asked how it was that his flocks seemed so much to excel all others. At last he told the secret—"I give my principal attention to the lambs." Now, you elders of the church, and you my matronly sisters, you that know the Lord, and have known him for years, look up the lambs, search them out, and take a special care of them; and if they are well nurtured in their early days, they will get a strength of spiritual constitution that will make them the joy of the Good Shepherd during the rest of their days. Now I leave that point.

III

In the second place, I said that I would address a word or two to feeble workers. Thank God, there are many workers here tonight, and maybe they will put themselves down as feeble. May the words I utter be an encouragement to them, and to feeble workers collectively. When a church begins, it is usually small, and the day of small things is a time of considerable anxiety and fear. I may be addressing some who are members of a newly organized church. Dear brethren, do not despise the day of small things. Rest assured that God does not save by numbers, and that results are not in the spiritual kingdom in proportion to numbers.

I have been reading lately with considerable care the life of John Wesley by two or three different authors in order to get, as well as I could, a fair idea of the good man; but one thing I have noticed: that the beginnings of the work that has become so wonderfully large were very small indeed. Mr. Wesley and his first brethren were not rich people. Nearly all that joined him were poor. Here and there, there was a person of some standing, but the Methodists were the poor of the land. And his first preachers were not men of education. One or two were so, but the most were good outdoor preachers—head preachers, magnificent preachers as God made them by his Spirit; but they were not men who had had the benefit of college training or who were remarkable for ability. The Methodists had neither money nor eminent men at first, and their numbers were very few. During the whole life of that good man, which was protracted for so many years, the denomination did not attain any very remarkable size. They were few, and apparently feeble; but Methodism was never so glorious as it was at first, and there never were so many conversions, I believe, as in those early days. Now, I speak sorrowfully. It is a great denomination. It abounds in wealth: I am glad it does. It has mighty orators: I rejoice it has. But it has no increase, no conversion. This year and other years it remains stationary. I do not say this because that is an exceptional denomination, for almost all others have the same tale. Year by year as the statistics come in, it is just this: "No increase—hardly hold our ground."

I use that as an illustration here. This church will get in precisely the same condition if we do not look out—just the same state. When we have not the means, we get the blessing, and when we seem to have the might and power, then the blessing does not come. Oh! may God send us poverty; may God send us lack of means, and take away our power of speech if it must be, and help us only to stammer, if we may only thus get the blessing. Oh! I crave to be useful to souls, and all the rest may go where it will. And each church must crave the same. "Not by might, nor by power, but by my spirit, saith the LORD" (Zech. 4:6). Instead of despising the day of small things, we ought to be encouraged. It is by the small things that God seems to work, but the great things he does not often use. He won't have Gideon's great host: let them go to their homes—let the mass of them go. Bring them down to the water: pick out only the men that lap, and then there is a very few. You can tell them almost on your fingers' ends—just two or three hundred men. Then Gideon shall go forth against the Midianites; and as the cake of barley bread smote the tent, and it lay along, so the sound of the sword of the Lord and of Gideon at the dead of night shall make the host to tremble, and the Lord God shall get to himself the victory. Never mind your feebleness, brethren, your fewness, your poverty, your want of ability. Throw your souls into God's cause, pray mightily, lay hold on the gates of heaven, stir heaven and earth rather than be defeated in winning souls, and you will see results that will astonish you yet. "Who hath despised the day of small things?"

Now take the case of each Christian individually. Every one of us ought to be at work for Christ, but the great mass of us cannot do great things. Don't despise, then, the day of little things. You can only give a penny. Now then, he that sat over by the treasury did not despise the widow's two mites that made a farthing. Your little thank offering, if given from your heart, is as acceptable as if it had been a hundred times as much. Don't, therefore, neglect to do the little. Don't despise the day of small things. You can only give away a tract in the street. Don't say, "I won't do that." Souls have been saved by the distribution of tracts and sermons. Scatter them, scatter them—they will be good seed. You know not where they may fall. You can only write a letter to a friend about Christ. Don't neglect to do it: write one tomorrow. Remember a playmate of yours; you may take liberties with him about his soul from your intimacy with him. Write to him about his state before God and urge him to seek the Savior. Who knows?—a sermon may miss him, but a letter from the well-known school companion will reach his heart. Mother, it is only two or three little children at home that you have an influence over. Despise not the day of small things. Take them tomorrow; put your arms around their necks as they kneel by you—pray, "God bless my boys and girls, and save them"—and tell them of Christ now. Oh! How well can mothers preach to children!

I can never forget my mother's teaching. On Sunday night, when we were at home, she would have us around the table and explain the Scriptures as we read, and then pray; and one night she left an impression upon my mind that never will be erased, when she said, "I have told you, my dear children, the way of salvation, and if you perish you will perish justly. I shall have to say 'Amen' to your condemnation if you are condemned"; and I could not bear that. Anybody else might say, "Amen," but not my mother. Oh! You don't know—you that have to deal with children—what you may do.

Despise not these little opportunities. Put a word in edgeways for Christ—you that go about in trains, you that go into workshops and factories. If Christians were men who were all true to their colors, I think we should soon see a great change come over our great establishments. Speak up for Jesus—be not ashamed of him, and because you can say but little, don't refuse, therefore, to say that, but rather say it over twenty times, and so make the little into much. Again, and again, and again, repeat the feeble stroke, and there shall come to be as much result from it as from one tremendous blow. God accepts your little works if they are done in faith in his dear Son. God will give success to your little works: God will educate you by your little works to do greater works; and your little works may call out others who shall do greater works by far than ever you shall be able to accomplish. Evangelists, go on preaching at the street corner—you that visit the low lodging houses, go on. Get into the room and talk of Jesus

Christ there as you have done. You that go into the country towns on the Sabbath and speak on the village greens of Christ, go on with it. I am glad to see you, but I am glad to miss you when I know you are about the Master's work. We don't want to keep the salt in the box: let it be rubbed into the putrid mass to stay the putrification. We don't want the seed forever in the corn bin: let it be scattered, and it will give us more. Oh! brethren and sisters, wake up if any of you are asleep. Don't let an ounce of strength in this church be wasted—not a single grain of ability, either in the way of doing, or praying, or giving, or holy living. Spend and be spent, for who hath despised the day of small things? The Lord encourage weak believers, and the Lord accept the efforts of feeble workers, and send to both his richest benediction for Christ's sake. Amen.

THE MINISTER'S
FAINTING FITS

I

AS IT IS RECORDED THAT DAVID, in the heat of battle, waxed faint, so may it be written of all the servants of the Lord. Fits of depression come over the most of us. Usually cheerful as we may be, we must at intervals be cast down. The strong are not always vigorous, the wise not always ready, the brave not always courageous, and the joyous not always happy. There may be here and there men of iron, to whom wear and tear work no perceptible detriment, but surely the rust frets even these; and as for ordinary men, the Lord knows, and makes them to know, that they are but dust. Knowing by most painful experience what deep depression of spirit means, being visited therewith at seasons by no means few or far between, I thought it might be consolatory to some of my brethren if I gave my thoughts thereon, that younger men might not fancy that some strange thing had happened to them when they became for a season possessed by melancholy; and that sadder men might know that one upon whom the sun has shone right joyously did not always walk in the light.

It is not necessary by quotations from the biographies of eminent ministers to prove that seasons of fearful prostration have fallen to the lot of most, if not all, of them. The life of Martin Luther might suffice to give a thousand instances, and he was by no means of the weaker sort. His great spirit was often in the seventh heaven of exultation and as frequently on the borders of despair. His very deathbed was not free from tempests, and he sobbed himself into his last sleep like a great wearied child. Instead of multiplying cases, let us dwell upon the reasons why these things are permitted; why it is that the children of light sometimes walk in the thick darkness; why the heralds of the daybreak find themselves at times in tenfold night.

Is it not first that they are men? Being men, they are compassed with infirmity, and are heirs of sorrow. Well said the wise man in the Apocrypha,

Great travail is created for all men, and a heavy yoke on the sons of Adam, from the day that they go out of their mother's womb unto that day that they return to the mother of all things—namely, their thoughts and fear of their hearts, and their imagination of things that they wail for, and the day of death. From him that sitteth in the glorious throne, to him that sitteth beneath in the earth and ashes; from him that is clothed in blue silk and weareth a crown, to him that is clothed in simple linen—wrath, envy, trouble, and unquietness, and fear of death and rigor, . . . and such things come to both man and beast, but sevenfold to the ungodly. (Sir. 40:1–8)

Grace guards us from much of this, but because we have not more of grace, we still suffer even from ills preventable. Even under the economy of redemption, it is most clear that we are to endure infirmities—otherwise there were no need of the promised Spirit to help us in them. It is of need be that we are sometimes in heaviness. Good men are promised tribulation in this world, and ministers may expect a larger share than others, that they may learn sympathy with the Lord's suffering people, and so may be fitting shepherds of an ailing flock. Disembodied spirits might have been sent to proclaim the word, but they could not have entered into the feelings of those who, being in this body, do groan, being burdened; angels might have been ordained evangelists, but their celestial attributes would have disqualified them from having compassion on the ignorant; men of marble might have been fashioned, but their impassive natures would have been a sarcasm upon our feebleness and a mockery of our wants. Men, and men subject to human passions, the all-wise God has chosen to be his vessels of grace; hence these tears, hence these perplexities and castings down.

Moreover, most of us are in some way or other unsound physically. Here and there we meet with an old man who could not remember that ever he was laid aside for a day; but the great mass of us labor under some form or other of infirmity, either in body or mind. Certain bodily maladies, especially those connected with the digestive organs, the liver, and the spleen, are the fruitful fountains of despondency; and, let a man strive as he may against their influence, there will be hours and circumstances in which they will, for awhile, overcome him. As to mental maladies, is any man altogether sane? Are we not all a little off the balance? Some minds appear to have a gloomy tinge essential to their very individuality; of them it may be said, "Melancholy marked them for her own"; fine minds withal, and ruled by noblest principles, but yet most prone to forget the silver lining and to remember only the cloud. Such men may sing with the old poet,

> Our hearts are broke, our harps unstringed be,
>   Our only music's sighs and groans.
> Our songs are to the tune of lachrymae,
>   We're fretted all to skin and bones.[3]

3   From "The Vine Wasted" by Thomas Washbourne, 1868.

These infirmities may be no detriment to a man's career of special usefulness; they may even have been imposed upon him by divine wisdom as necessary qualifications for his peculiar course of service. Some plants owe their medicinal qualities to the marsh in which they grow; others to the shades in which alone they flourish. There are precious fruits put forth by the moon as well as by the sun. Boats need ballast as well as sail; a drag on the carriage wheel is no hindrance when the road runs downhill. Pain has, probably, in some cases developed genius, hunting out the soul that otherwise might have slept like a lion in its den. Had it not been for the broken wing, some might have lost themselves in the clouds, some even of those choice doves who now bear the olive branch in their mouths and show the way to the ark. But where in body and mind there are predisposing causes to lowness of spirit, it is no marvel if in dark moments the heart succumbs to them; the wonder in many cases is—and if inner lives could be written, men would see it so—how some ministers keep at their work at all and still wear a smile upon their countenances. Grace has its triumphs still, and patience has its martyrs; martyrs none the less to be honored because the flames kindle about their spirits rather than their bodies, and their burning is unseen of human eyes. The ministries of Jeremiahs are as acceptable as those of Isaiahs, and even the sullen Jonah is a true prophet of the Lord, as Nineveh felt full well. Despise not the lame, for it is written that they take the prey (Isa. 33:23); but honor those who, being faint, are yet pursuing (Judg. 8:4). The tender-eyed Leah was more fruitful than the beautiful Rachel, and the griefs of Hannah were more divine than the boastings of Peninnah. "Blessed are they that mourn" (Matt. 5:4), said the man of sorrows, and let none account them otherwise when their tears are salted with grace. We have the treasure of the gospel in earthen vessels, and if there be a flaw in the vessel here and there, let none wonder.

II

Our work, when earnestly undertaken, lays us open to attacks in the direction of depression. Who can bear the weight of souls without sometimes sinking to the dust? Passionate longings after men's conversion, if not fully satisfied (and when are they?), consume the soul with anxiety and disappointment. To see the hopeful turn aside, the godly grow cold, professors abusing their privileges, and sinners waxing more bold in sin—are not these sights enough to crush us to the earth? The kingdom comes not as we would, the reverend name is not hallowed as we desire, and for this we must weep. How can we be otherwise than sorrowful while men believe not our report and the divine arm is not revealed? All mental work tends to weary and to depress, for much study is a weariness of the flesh; but ours is more than mental work—it is heart work, the labor of our inmost soul. How often, on Lord's Day evenings, do we feel as if life were completely washed out of us! After pouring out our souls over our congregations, we feel like empty earthen pitchers that a child might break. Probably, if we were more like Paul and watched for souls at a nobler rate, we should know more of what it is to be eaten up by the zeal of the Lord's house. It is our duty and our privilege to exhaust our lives for Jesus. We are not to be living specimens of men in fine preservation, but living sacrifices whose lot is to be consumed; we are to spend and to be spent, not to lay ourselves up in lavender and nurse our flesh. Such soul travail as that of a faithful minister will bring on occasional seasons of exhaustion, when heart and flesh will fail. Moses's hands grew heavy in intercession, and Paul cried out, "Who is sufficient for these things?" (2 Cor. 2:16). Even John the Baptist is thought to have had his fainting fits, and the apostles were once amazed and were sore afraid.

Our position in the church will also conduce to this. A minister fully equipped for his work will usually be a spirit by himself, above, beyond, and apart from others. The most loving of his people cannot enter into his peculiar thoughts, cares, and temptations. In the ranks, men walk shoulder to shoulder, with many comrades, but as the officer rises in rank, men of his standing are fewer in number. There are many soldiers, few captains, fewer colonels, but only one commander in chief. So, in our churches, the man whom the Lord raises as a leader becomes, in the same degree in which he is a superior man, a solitary man. The mountaintops stand solemnly apart and talk only with God as he visits their terrible solitudes. Men of God who rise above their fellows into nearer communion with heavenly things, in their weaker moments feel the lack of human sympathy. Like their Lord in Gethsemane, they look in vain for comfort to the disciples sleeping around them; they are shocked at the apathy of their little band of brethren and return to their secret agony with all the heavier burden pressing upon them because they have found their dearest companions slumbering. No one knows, but he who has endured it, the solitude of a soul that has outstripped its fellows in zeal for the Lord of hosts: it dares not reveal itself, lest men count it mad; it cannot conceal itself, for a fire burns within its bones; only before the Lord does it find rest. Our Lord's sending out his disciples by two and two manifested that he knew what was in men; but for such a man as Paul, it seems to me that no helpmeet was found: Barnabas, or Silas, or Luke were hills too low to hold high converse with such a Himalayan summit as the apostle of the Gentiles. This loneliness, which if I mistake not is felt by many of my brethren, is a fertile source of depression; and our ministers' fraternal meeting and the cultivation of holy intercourse with kindred minds will, with God's blessing, help us greatly to escape the snare.

There can be little doubt that sedentary habits have a tendency to create despondency in some constitutions. Robert Burton, in his *The Anatomy of Melancholy*, has a chapter upon this cause of sadness; quoting from one of the myriad authors whom he lays under contribution, he says, "Students are negligent of their bodies. Other men look to their tools; a painter will wash his pencils; a smith will look to his hammer, anvil, forge; a husbandman will mend his plough-irons, and grind his hatchet if it be dull; a falconer or huntsman will have an especial care of his hawks, hounds, horses, dogs, etc.; a musician will string and unstring his lute; only scholars neglect that instrument (their brain and spirits I mean) which they daily use. Well saith Lucan, 'See thou twist not the rope so hard that it break.'"[4] To sit long in one posture, poring over a book or driving a quill, is in itself a taxing of nature; but add to this a badly ventilated chamber, a body that has long been without muscular exercise, and a heart burdened with many cares,

---

4   From Robert Burton, *The Anatomy of Melancholy*, first published 1621. It is unclear which edition Spurgeon is quoting.

and we have all the elements for preparing a seething cauldron of despair, especially in the dim months of fog,

> When a blanket wraps the day,
> When the rotten woodland drips,
> And the leaf is stamped in clay.[5]

Let a man be naturally as blithe as a bird, he will hardly be able to bear up year after year against such a suicidal process; he will make his study a prison and his books the warders of a jail, while nature lies outside his window calling him to health and beckoning him to joy. He who forgets the humming of the bees among the heather, the cooing of the wood pigeons in the forest, the song of birds in the woods, the rippling of rills among the rushes, and the sighing of the

---

5 From "The Vision of Sin" by Alfred, Lord Tennyson, 1842.

wind among the pines needs not wonder if his heart forgets to sing and his soul grows heavy. A day's breathing of fresh air upon the hills or a few hours' ramble in the beech woods' umbrageous calm would sweep the cobwebs out of the brains of scores of our toiling ministers who are now but half alive. A mouthful of sea air or a stiff walk in the wind's face would not give grace to the soul, but it would yield oxygen to the body, which is next best.

> "Heaviest the heart is
> In a heavy air;
> Ev'ry wind that rises
> Blows away despair."[6]

The ferns and the rabbits, the streams and the trouts, the fir trees and the squirrels, the prim-

---

6   From "The Rivulet: Contribution to Sacred Song" by Thomas T. Lynch, 1868.

roses and the violets, the farmyard, the new-mown hay, and the fragrant hops—these are the best medicine for hypochondriacs, the surest tonics for the declining, the best refreshments for the weary. For lack of opportunity or inclination, these great remedies are neglected, and the student becomes a self-immolated victim.

III

The times most favorable to fits of depression, so far as I have experienced, may be summed up in a brief catalog. First among them I must mention the hour of great success. When at last a long-cherished desire is fulfilled, when God has been glorified greatly by our means and a great triumph achieved, then we are apt to faint. It might be imagined that amid special favors our soul would soar to heights of ecstasy and rejoice with joy unspeakable, but it is generally the reverse. The Lord seldom exposes his warriors to the perils of exultation over victory; he knows that few of them can endure such a test, and therefore dashes their cup with bitterness. See Elijah after the fire has fallen from heaven, Baal's priests have been slaughtered, and the rain has deluged the barren land! For him no notes of self-complacent music, no strutting like a conqueror in robes of triumph; he flees from Jezebel and, feeling the revulsion of his intense excitement, he prays that he may die. He who must never see death yearns after the rest of the grave, even as Caesar, the world's monarch, in his moments of pain cried like a sick girl. Poor human nature cannot bear such strains as heavenly triumphs bring to it; there must come a reaction. Excess of joy or excitement must be paid for by subsequent depressions. While the trial lasts, the strength is equal to the emergency;

but when it is over, natural weakness claims the right to show itself. Secretly sustained, Jacob can wrestle all night, but he must limp in the morning when the contest is over lest he boast himself beyond measure. Paul may be caught up to the third heaven and hear unspeakable things, but a thorn in the flesh, a messenger of Satan to buffet him, must be the inevitable sequel. Men cannot bear unalloyed happiness; even good men are not yet fit to have "their brows with laurel and with myrtle bound" without enduring secret humiliation to keep them in their proper place. Whirled off our feet by a revival, carried aloft by popularity, exalted by success in soul winning, we should be as the chaff that the wind driveth away were it not that the gracious discipline of mercy breaks the ships of our vainglory with a strong east wind and casts us shipwrecked, naked and forlorn, upon the Rock of Ages.

Before any great achievement, some measure of the same depression is very usual. Surveying the difficulties before us, our hearts sink within us. The sons of Anak stalk before us, and we are as grasshoppers in our own sight in their presence. The cities of Canaan are walled up to heaven, and who are we that we should hope to capture them? We are ready to cast down our weapons and take to our heels. Nineveh is a great city, and we would flee unto Tarshish sooner than encounter its noisy crowds. Already we look for a ship that may bear us quietly away from the terrible scene, and only a dread of tempest restrains our recreant footsteps.

Such was my experience when I first became a pastor in London. My success appalled me; and the thought of the career that it seemed to open up, so far from elating me, cast me into the lowest depth, out of which I uttered my miserere and found no room for a gloria in excelsis. Who was I that I should continue to lead so great a multitude? I would betake me to my village obscurity, or emigrate to America, and find a solitary nest in the backwoods where I might be sufficient for the things that would be demanded of me. It was just then that the curtain was rising upon my life work, and I dreaded what it might reveal. I hope I was not faithless, but I was timorous and filled with a sense of my own unfitness. I dreaded the work that a gracious providence had prepared for me. I felt myself a mere child, and trembled as I heard the voice that said, "Arise, and thresh the mountains, and make them as chaff."[7] This depression comes over me whenever the Lord is preparing a larger blessing for my ministry; the cloud is black before it breaks, and overshadows

7 See Isa. 41:15.

before it yields its deluge of mercy. Depression has now become to me as a prophet in rough clothing, a John the Baptist heralding the nearer coming of my Lord's richer benison. So have far better men found it. The scouring of the vessel has fitted it for the Master's use. Immersion in suffering has preceded the baptism of the Holy Ghost. Fasting gives an appetite for the banquet. The Lord is revealed in the backside of the desert, while his servant keepeth the sheep and waits in solitary awe. The wilderness is the way to Canaan. The low valley leads to the towering mountain. Defeat prepares for victory. The raven is sent forth before the dove. The darkest hour of the night precedes the day dawn. The mariners go down to the depths, but the next wave makes them mount to the heaven: their soul is melted because of trouble before he bringeth them to their desired haven.

In the midst of a long stretch of unbroken labor, the same affliction may be looked for. The bow cannot be always bent without fear of breaking. Repose is as needful to the mind as sleep to the body. Our Sabbaths are our days of toil, and if we do not rest upon some other day, we shall break down. Even the earth must lie fallow and have her Sabbaths, and so must we. Hence the wisdom and compassion of our Lord, when he said to his disciples, "Let us go into the desert and rest awhile."[8] What! when the people are fainting? When the multitudes are like sheep upon the mountains without a shepherd? Does Jesus talk of rest? When scribes and Pharisees, like grievous wolves, are rending the flock, does he take his followers on an excursion into a quiet resting place? Does some red-hot zealot denounce such

8   See Mark 6:31.

atrocious forgetfulness of present and pressing demands? Let him rave in his folly. The Master knows better than to exhaust his servants and quench the light of Israel. Rest time is not waste time. It is economy to gather fresh strength. Look at the mower in the summer's day, with so much to cut down ere the sun sets. He pauses in his labor—is he a sluggard? He looks for his stone and begins to draw it up and down his scythe, with "rink-a-tink—rink-a-tink—rink-a-tink." Is that idle music—is he wasting precious moments? How much he might have mown while he has been ringing out those notes on his scythe! But he is sharpening his tool, and he will do far more when once again he gives his strength to those long sweeps that lay the grass prostrate in rows before him. Even thus a little pause prepares the mind for greater service in the good cause. Fishermen must mend their nets, and we must, every now and then, repair our mental waste and set our machinery in order for future service. To tug the oar from day to day, like a galley slave who knows no holidays, suits not mortal men. Millstreams go on and on forever, but we must have our pauses and our intervals. Who can help being out of breath when the race is continued without intermission? Even beasts of burden must be turned out to grass occasionally; the very sea pauses at ebb and flood; earth keeps the Sabbath of the wintry months; and man, even when exalted to be God's ambassador, must rest or faint; must trim his lamp or let it burn low; must recruit his vigor or grow prematurely old. It is wisdom to take occasional furlough. In the long run, we shall do more by sometimes doing less. On, on, on forever, without recreation, may suit spirits emancipated from this "heavy clay," but while we are in this tabernacle, we must every now and then cry halt and serve the Lord by holy inaction and consecrated leisure. Let no tender conscience doubt the lawfulness of going out of harness for awhile, but learn from the experience of others the necessity and duty of taking timely rest.

One crushing stroke has sometimes laid the minister very low. The brother most relied upon becomes a traitor. Judas lifts up his heel against the man who trusted him, and the preacher's heart for the moment fails him. We are all too apt to look to an arm of flesh, and from that propensity many of our sorrows arise. Equally overwhelming is the blow when an honored and beloved member yields to temptation and disgraces the holy name with which he was named. Anything is better than this. This makes the preacher long for a lodge in some vast wilderness, where he may hide his head forever and hear no more the blasphemous jeers of the ungodly.

Ten years of toil do not take so much life out of us as we lose in a few hours by Ahithophel the traitor or Demas the apostate. Strife, also, and division, slander, and foolish censures have often laid holy men prostrate and made them go "as with a sword in their bones."[9] Hard words wound some delicate minds very keenly. Many of the best of ministers, from the very spirituality of their character, are exceedingly sensitive—too sensitive for such a world as this. "A kick that scarce would move a horse would kill a sound divine."[10] By experience the soul is hardened to the rough blows that are inevitable in our warfare, but at first these things utterly stagger us and send us to our homes wrapped in a horror of great darkness. The trials of a true minister are not few, and such as are caused by ungrateful professors are

9 See Ps. 42:10.
10 From William Cowper, "The Yearly Distress," 1779.

harder to bear than the coarsest attacks of avowed enemies. Let no man who looks for ease of mind and seeks the quietude of life enter the ministry; if he does so, he will flee from it in disgust.

To the lot of few does it fall to pass through such a horror of great darkness as that which fell upon me after the deplorable accident at the Surrey Music Hall. I was pressed beyond measure and out of bounds with an enormous weight of misery. The tumult, the panic, the deaths were day and night before me, and made life a burden. Then I sang in my sorrow,

> The tumult of my thoughts
>   Doth but increase my woe,
> My spirit languisheth, my heart
>   Is desolate and low.

From that dream of horror I was awakened in a moment by the gracious application to my soul of the text, "Him hath God the Father exalted."[11] The fact that Jesus is still great, let his servants suffer as they may, piloted me back to calm reason and peace. Should so terrible a calamity overtake any of my brethren, let them both patiently hope and quietly wait for the salvation of God.

IV

When troubles multiply, and discouragements follow each other in long succession, like Job's messengers, then, too, amid the perturbation of soul occasioned by evil tidings, despondency despoils the heart of all its peace. Constant dropping wears away stones, and the bravest minds feel the fret of repeated afflictions. If a scanty cupboard is rendered a severer trial by

11 See Phil. 2:9.

the sickness of a wife or the loss of a child, and if ungenerous remarks of hearers are followed by the opposition of deacons and the coolness of members, then, like Jacob, we are apt to cry, "All these things are against me" (Gen. 42:36). When David returned to Ziklag and found the city burned, goods stolen, wives carried off, and his troops ready to stone him, we read, "David encouraged himself in the LORD his God" (1 Sam. 30:6), and well was it for him that he could do so, for he would then have fainted if he had not believed to see the goodness of the Lord in the land of the living (see Ps. 27:13). Accumulated distresses increase each other's weight; they play into each other's hands, and, like bands of robbers, ruthlessly destroy our comfort. Wave upon wave is severe work for the strongest swimmer. The place where two seas meet strains the most seaworthy keel. If there were a regulated pause between the buffetings of adversity, the spirit would stand prepared; but when they come suddenly and heavily, like the battering of great hailstones, the pilgrim may well be amazed. The last ounce breaks the camel's back, and when that last ounce is laid upon us, what wonder if we, for awhile, are ready to give up the ghost!

This evil will also come upon us, we know not why, and then it is all the more difficult to drive it away. Causeless depression is not to be reasoned with, nor can David's harp charm it away by sweet discoursings. As well fight with the mist as with this shapeless, undefinable, yet all-beclouding hopelessness. One affords himself no pity when in this case, because it seems so unreasonable, and even sinful, to be troubled without manifest cause; and yet troubled the man is, even in the very depths of his spirit. If those who laugh at such melancholy did but feel the grief of it for one hour, their laughter would be sobered into compassion. Resolution might, perhaps, shake it off, but where are we to find the resolution when the whole man is unstrung? The physician and the divine may unite their skill in such cases, and both find their hands full, and more than full. The iron bolt that so mysteriously fastens the door of hope and holds our spirits in gloomy prison needs a heavenly hand to push it back; and when that hand is seen, we cry with the apostle, "Blessed be God, even the Father of our Lord Jesus Christ, the Father of mercies, and the God of all comfort; who comforteth us in all our tribulation, that we may be able to comfort them which are in any trouble, by the comfort wherewith we ourselves are comforted of God" (2 Cor. 1:3–4). It is the God of all consolation who can

With sweet oblivious antidote
Cleanse our poor bosoms of that perilous
    stuff
Which weighs upon the heart.[12]

Simon sinks till Jesus takes him by the hand. The devil within rends and tears the poor child till the word of authority commands him to come out of him. When we are ridden with horrible fears and weighed down with an intolerable incubus, we need but the Sun of Righteousness to rise, and the evils generated of our darkness are driven away; but nothing short of this will chase away the nightmare of the soul. Timothy Rogers, the author of a treatise on melancholy, and Simon Browne, the writer of some remarkably sweet hymns, proved in their own cases how unavailing is the help of man if the Lord withdraw the light from the soul.

12   From William Shakespeare, "Macbeth," Act 5, Scene 3.

If it be inquired why the valley of the shadow of death must so often be traversed by the servants of King Jesus, the answer is not far to find. All this is promotive of the Lord's mode of working, which is summed up in these words: "Not by might, nor by power, but by my spirit, saith the LORD" (Zech. 4:6). Instruments shall be used, but their intrinsic weakness shall be clearly manifested; there shall be no division of the glory, no diminishing the honor due to the Great Worker. The man shall be emptied of self and then filled with the Holy Ghost. In his own apprehension, he shall be like a sere leaf driven of the tempest, and then shall be strengthened into a brazen wall against the enemies of truth. To hide pride from the worker is the great difficulty. Uninterrupted success and unfading joy in it would be more than our weak heads could bear. Our wine must needs be mixed with water, lest it turn our brains. My witness is that those who are honored of their Lord in public have usually to endure a secret chastening or to carry a peculiar cross, lest by any means they exalt themselves and fall into the snare of the devil. How constantly the Lord calls Ezekiel "Son of man"! Amid his soarings into the superlative splendors, just when with eye undimmed he is strengthened to gaze into the excellent glory, the word "Son of man" falls on his ears, sobering the heart that else might have been intoxicated with the honor conferred upon it. Such humbling but salutary messages our depressions whisper in our ears; they tell us in a manner not to be mistaken that we are but men, frail, feeble, apt to faint.

By all the castings down of his servants God is glorified, for they are led to magnify him when again he sets them on their feet, and even while prostrate in the dust their faith yields him praise. They speak all the more sweetly of his faithfulness and are the more firmly established in his love. Such mature men, as some elderly preachers are, could scarcely have been produced if they had not been emptied from vessel to vessel and made to see their own emptiness and the vanity of all things round about them. Glory be to God for the furnace, the hammer, and the file. Heaven shall be all the fuller of bliss because we have been filled with anguish here below, and earth shall be better tilled because of our training in the school of adversity.

The lesson of wisdom is, be not dismayed by soul trouble. Count it no strange thing, but a part of ordinary ministerial experience. Should the power of depression be more than ordinary, think not that all is over with your usefulness. Cast not away your confidence, for it hath great recompense of reward. Even if the enemy's foot be on your neck, expect to rise and overthrow him.

Cast the burden of the present, along with the sin of the past and the fear of the future, upon the Lord, who forsaketh not his saints. Live by the day—aye, by the hour. Put no trust in frames and feelings. Care more for a grain of faith than a ton of excitement. Trust in God alone and lean not on the reeds of human help. Be not surprised when friends fail you: it is a failing world. Never count upon immutability in man: inconstancy you may reckon upon without fear of disappointment. The disciples of Jesus forsook him; be not amazed if your adherents wander away to other teachers: as they were not your all when with you, all is not gone from you with their departure. Serve God with all your might while the candle is burning, and then when it goes out for a season, you will have the less to regret. Be content to be nothing, for that is what you are. When your own emptiness is painfully forced upon your consciousness, chide yourself that you ever dreamed of being full, except in the Lord. Set small store by present rewards; be grateful for earnests by the way, but look for the recompensing joy hereafter. Continue, with double earnestness, to serve your Lord when no visible result is before you. Any simpleton can follow the narrow path in the light: faith's rare wisdom enables us to march on in the dark with infallible accuracy, since she places her hand in that of her Great Guide. Between this and heaven there may be rougher weather yet, but it is all provided for by our covenant Head. In nothing let us be turned aside from the path that the divine call has urged us to pursue. Come fair or come foul, the pulpit is our watchtower and the ministry our warfare; be it ours, when we cannot see the face of our God, to trust under the shadow of his wings.

Scripture Index